The Cartoonists
Field Guide to the Birds
of New York City,
North America, and Beyond

Featuring Cartoons From
Air Mail
Esquire
The New Yorker
and more!

Front Cover illustration: Mort Gerberg
Back Cover illustration: Julia Suits
Introduction: Bob Mankoff
Edited By: Darren Kornblut

Dedicated to Jennifer & Bea

Cartoon Collections, LLC
10 Grand Central, 29th Floor
New York, NY 10017

For cartoon licensing information visit www.cartoonstock.com
Create a personalized version of this book at www.cartoonstockgifts.com

First edition published 2024

Item # 49184
ISBN: 978-1-963079-18-0

Introduction

Bird lovers and avid birdwatchers, gather 'round, for within the pages of this enchanting compilation lies a celebration of our shared passion—the marvelous world of birds and the joyous pursuit of observing them in their natural habitat. Welcome to a delightful collection of avian cartoons that will surely tickle your fancy and ignite your passion for the avian realm.

In this captivating journey, we find ourselves immersed in the wondrous world of our feathered companions, where they captivate our hearts with their graceful flight and enchanting melodies. However, as we explore these whimsical cartoons, we come to realize that the birds may be watching us as much as we watch them.

Through the strokes of talented cartoonists, we witness birds engaging in amusing antics, navigating the peculiarities of birdwatching enthusiasts, and highlighting the humorous aspects of this beloved pastime. From the keen gaze of birdwatchers to the humorous moments of mistaken identities and unexpected avian behaviors, these cartoons capture the essence of birdwatching with wit and charm.

So, whether you're a seasoned birdwatcher or a newcomer to the avian realm, prepare to be entertained and enlightened. Let us celebrate the beauty of birds, the joy of observation, and the humor that accompanies our feathered friends. May these cartoons bring a smile to your face and a renewed appreciation for the delightful world of birds and birdwatching

"*Good luck getting a sandwich at this hour in L.A.*"

"*No need to push, Mother—I'm going.*"

"It's only fair. He has a man cave."

"Now that's she mastered martinis,
let's move on to daquiris."

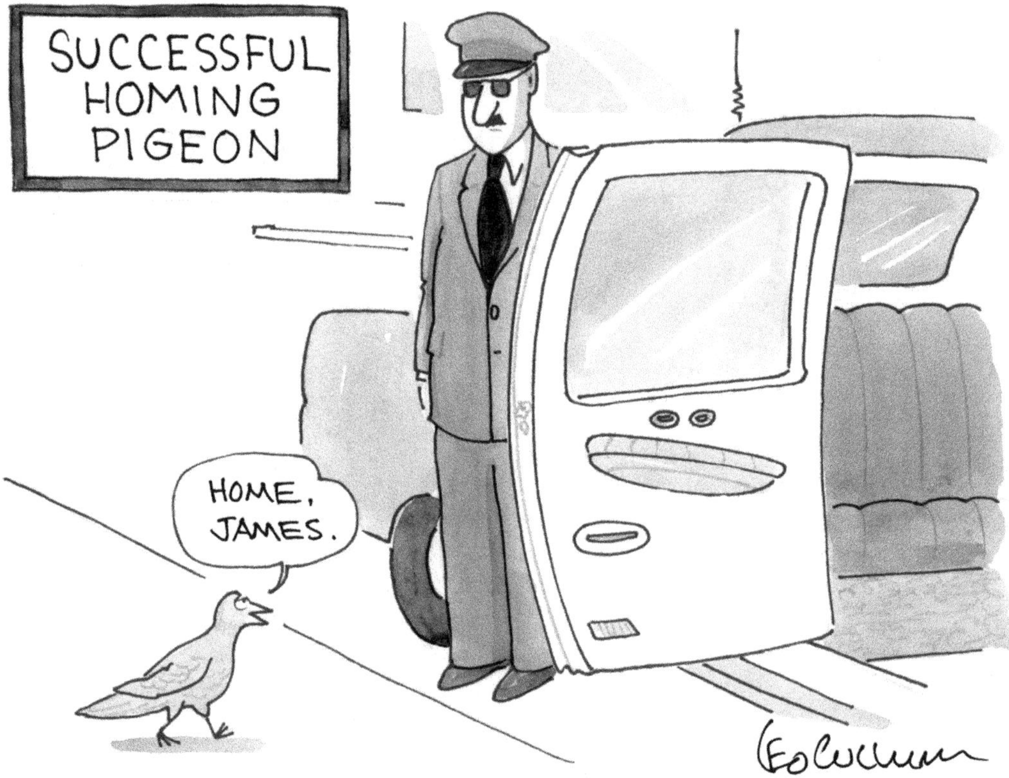
SUCCESSFUL
HOMING
PIGEON
HOME, JAMES.

"It's the best thing since bread torn into little pieces."

"I belonged to the Audubon Society."

"I never get tired of watching them."

"*According to Gaggle Maps we are on the fastest route possible.*"

"Trust me, this place is worth the wait."

"Of course I love you—I'm <u>programmed</u> to love you.
I'm a goddam <u>lovebird</u>."

"Actually, I'm a singer-songwriter bird."

SONGBIRD

RECORD
LABEL
BIRD

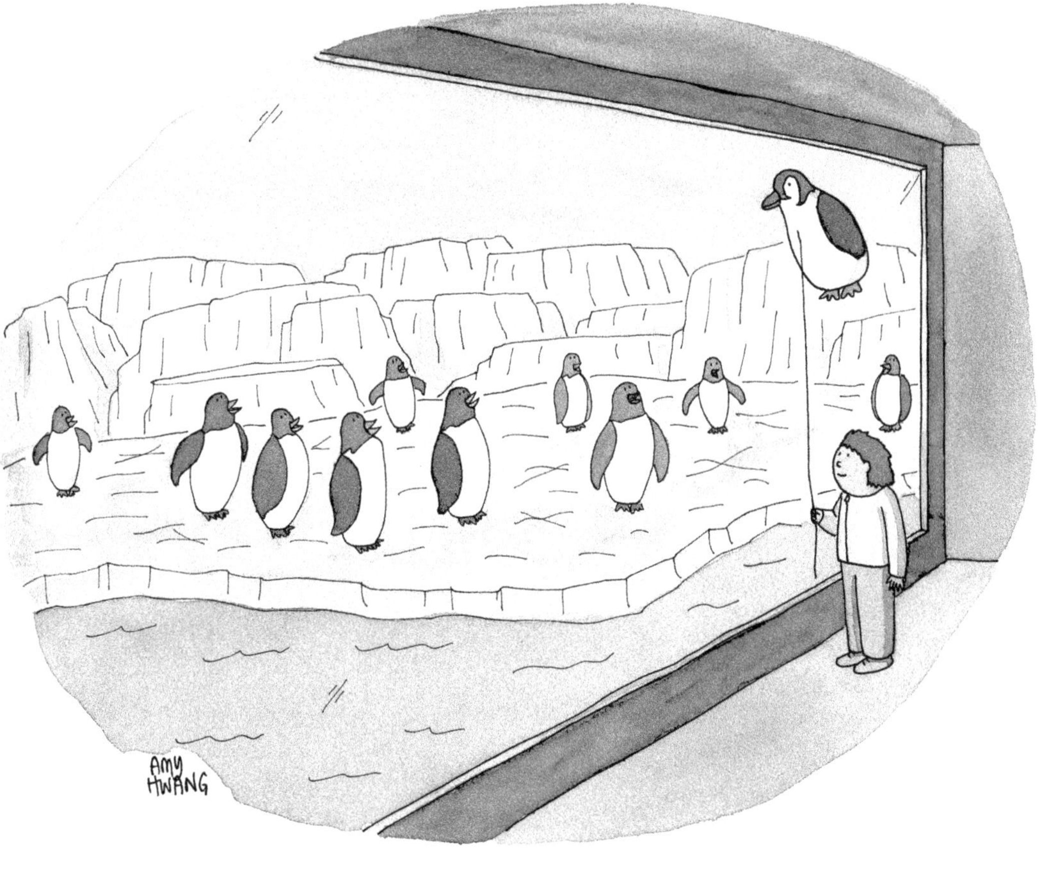
AMY
HWANG

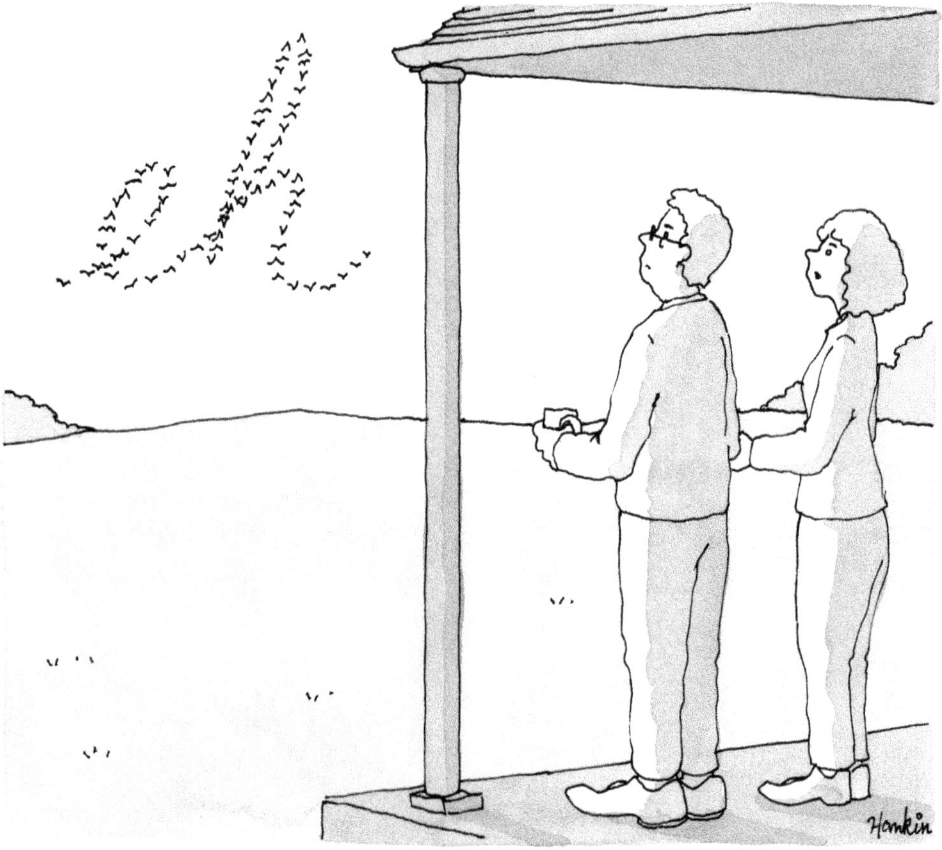
Hankin

"Canada geese."

"I fly south for the winter, and north for the bagels!"

"My mom's vomit. How 'bout you?"

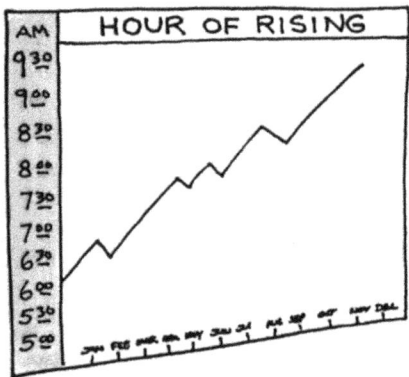

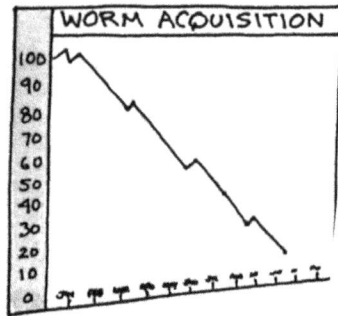

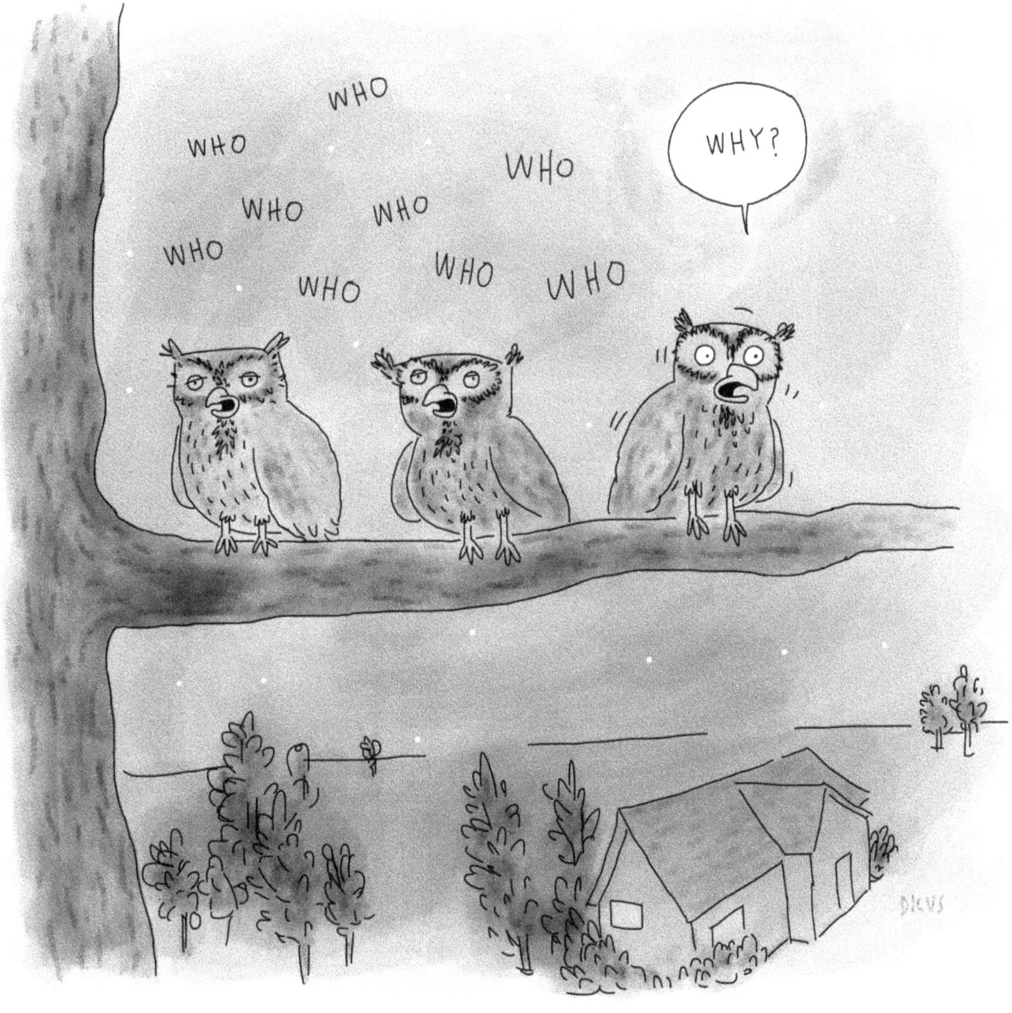
WHO
WHO
WHO
WHO
WHO
WHO
WHO
WHO
WHO
WHY?

LIANA
FINCK

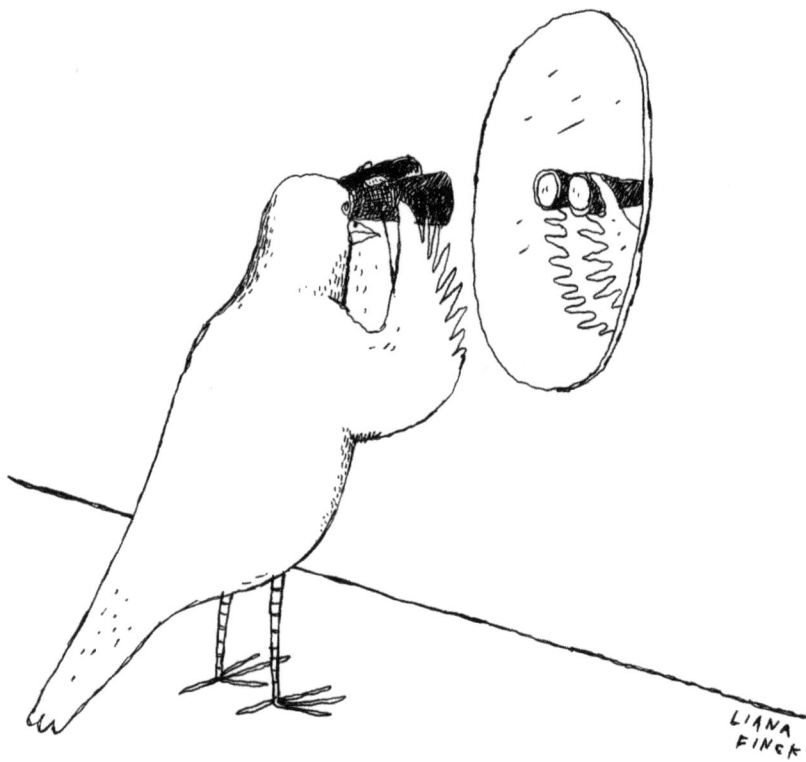

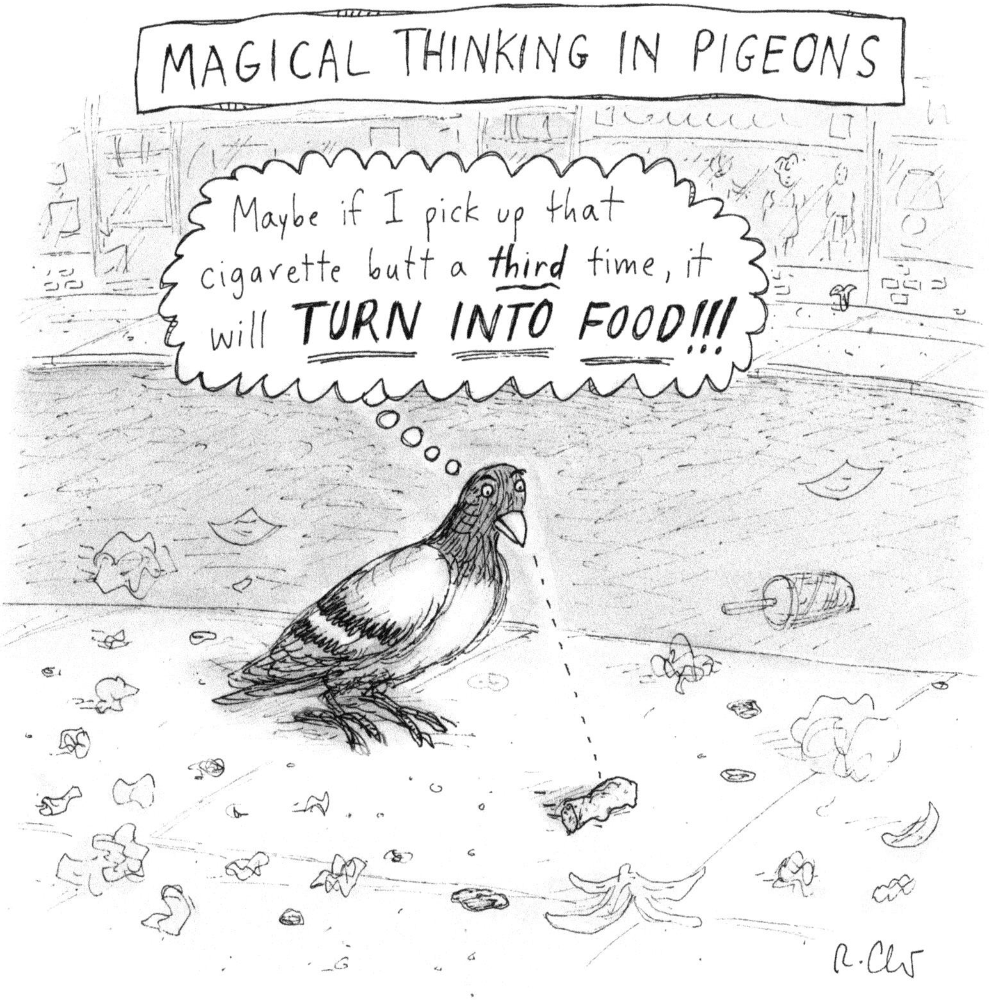
MAGICAL THINKING IN PIGEONS
Maybe if I pick up that cigarette butt a third time, it will TURN INTO FOOD!!!
R. Chast

"May I recommend the pumpkin seeds to start?"

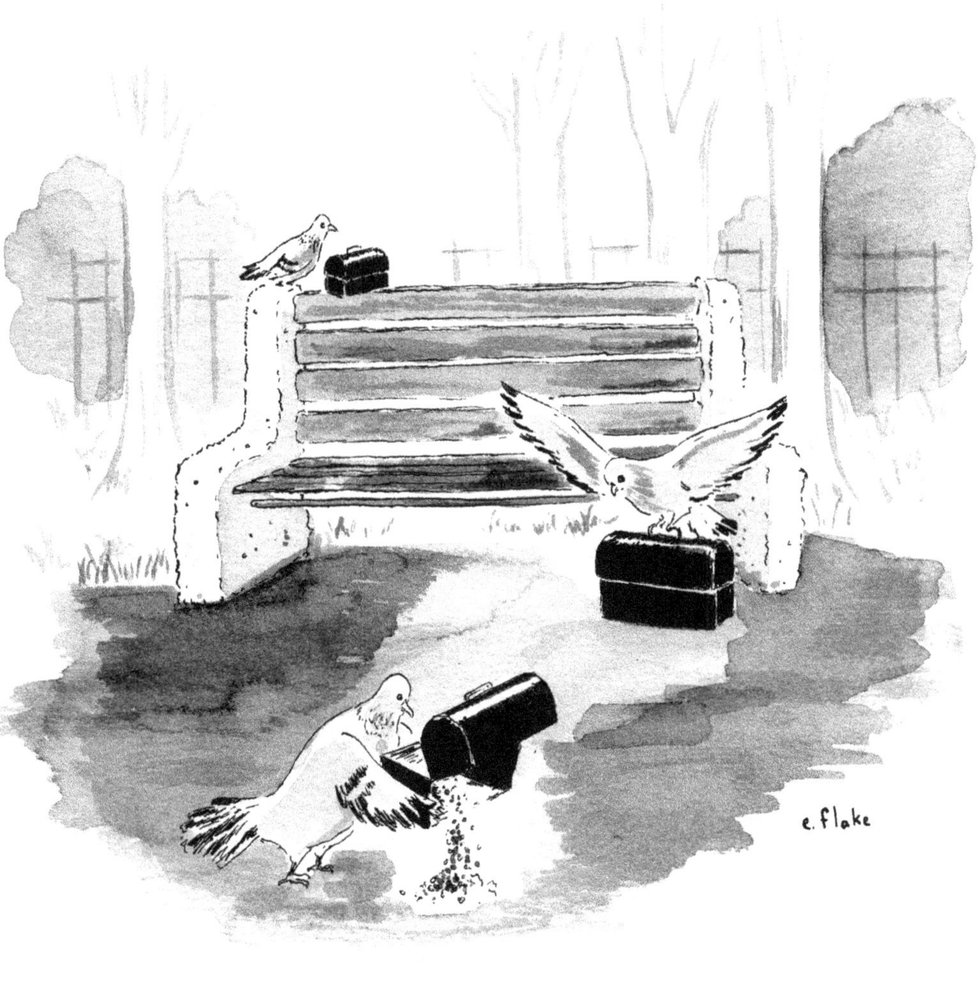
e. flake

"Maybe it doesn't want to be identified."

"Let me guess—you stayed late at your buddy's
place helping him with a, quoth, poem."

26

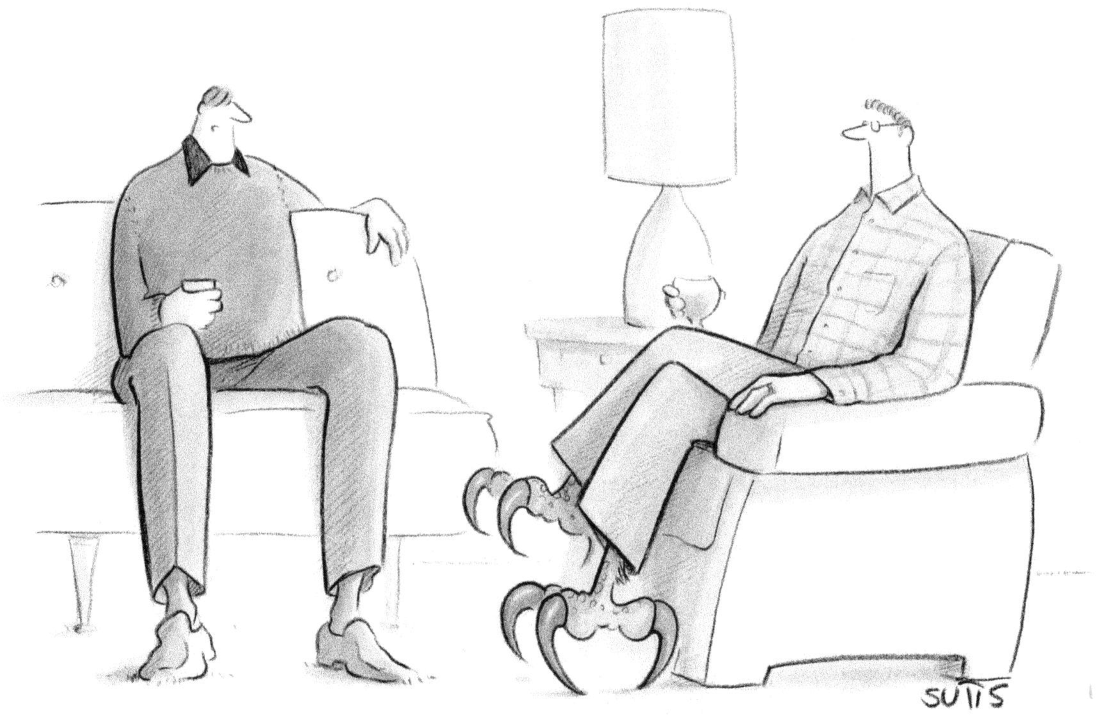
SUTIS

"Bob tells me you hunt."

"It's like I'm actually walking."

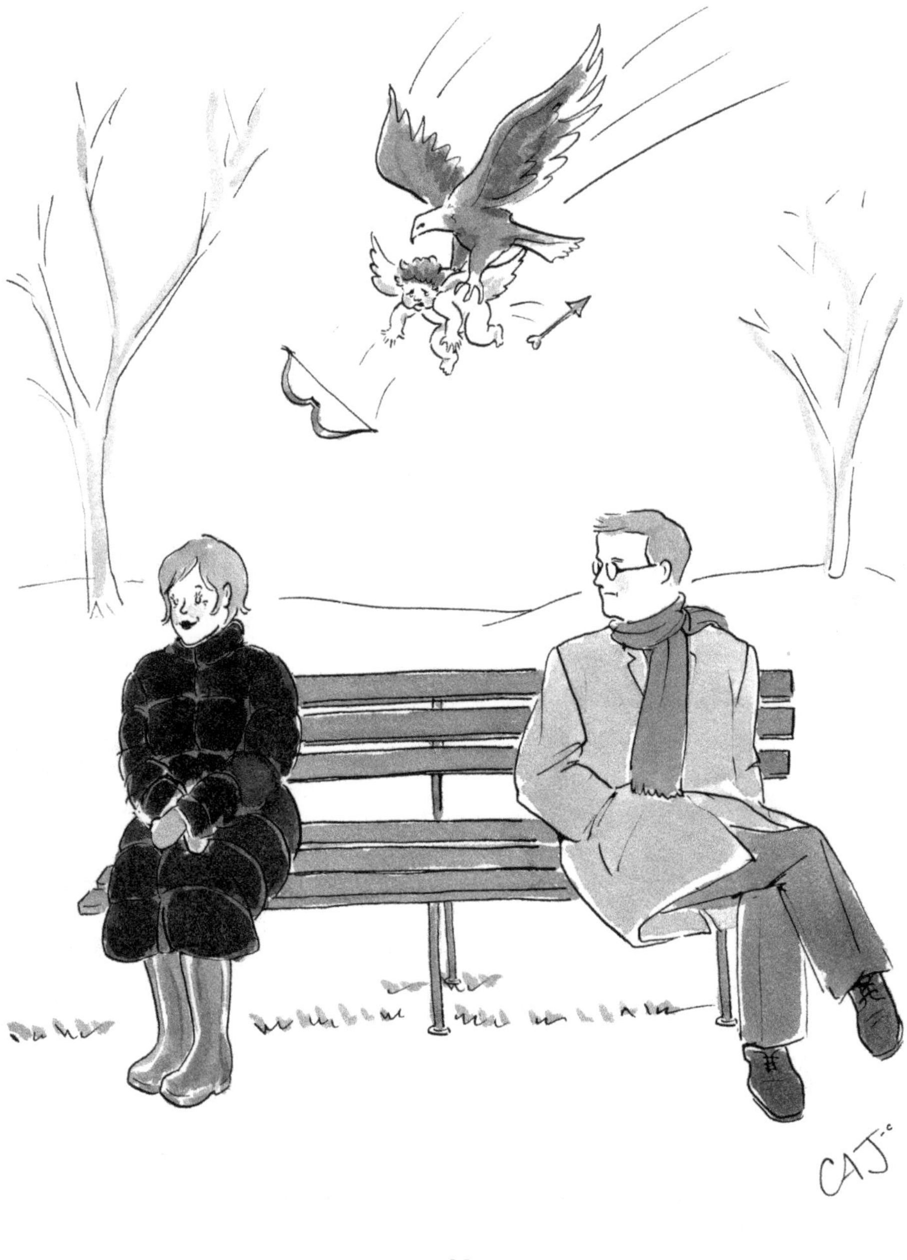
CAJ

"We need to create more hashtag-worthy moments."

"*And tomorrow I'll teach you how to build a nest.*"

"You'll be flying away soon, but wherever you go,
we want you to always remember you're the Connecticut state bird."

*"Of course you get good reception,
this is a cell phone tower."*

"I'm not spending another cent on birdseed."

"What's the big deal about outdoor dining?"

"*Mom and Dad have to migrant now, so we're leaving you with the au pair.*"

"*Please be spaghetti, please be spaghetti, please be spaghetti...*"

"*Frankly, I don't see the resemblance.*"

"We just haven't been flapping them hard enough."

"I just got damn well fed up with being formal all the time."

"They're totally cheating."

"Isn't that cute! They're thanking us."

"One large with pepperoni and mushrooms."

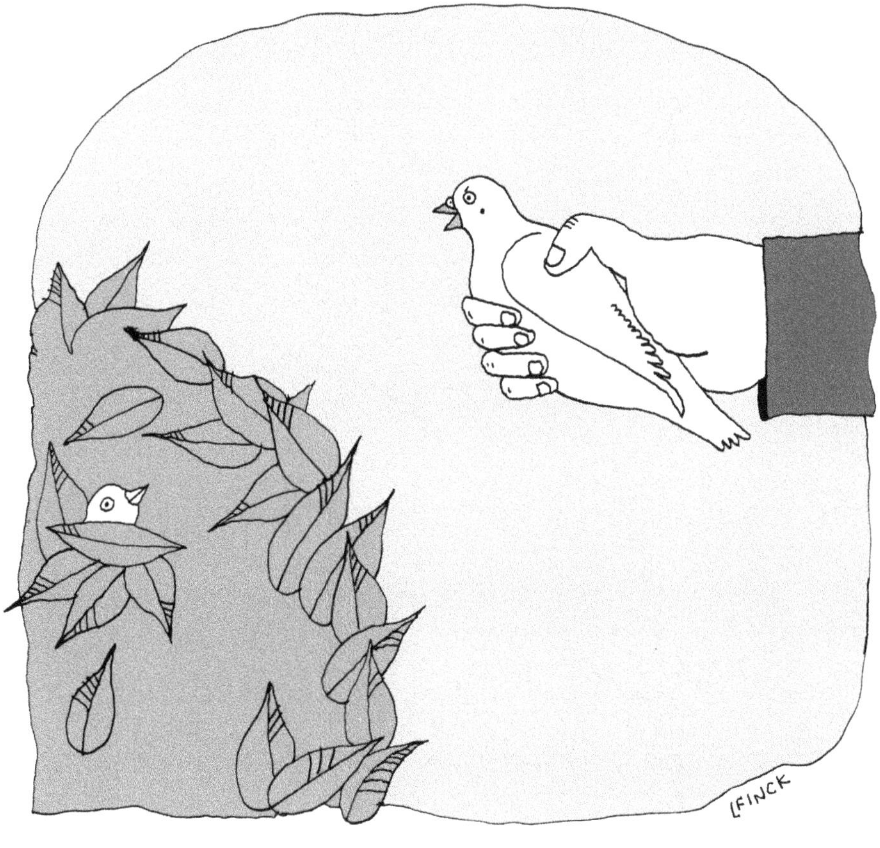
LFINCK

"My situation may not be the greatest, but I'll tell you this – I'm worth two of you!"

WILL SANTINO

"Don't forget—grubs, mites, worms. I want this
to be a _very_ special evening."

"YOU tell him he can't be our leader."

"*It's either extremely innovative or extremely stupid.*"

"Yes, as far as I know, songbirds write their own material."

"There's always one annoying piece left over."

"Working at home has been a mixed blessing."

"Oh, Julius, look! It's the first robin!"

"I'm sorry, I can't help you—you're subject to bird law now."

"Movies...snacks....what took us so long?"

"I love portraiture but my true calling is aerial photography."

"I can sleep late, but, as his agent, I still get ten percent of the worm."

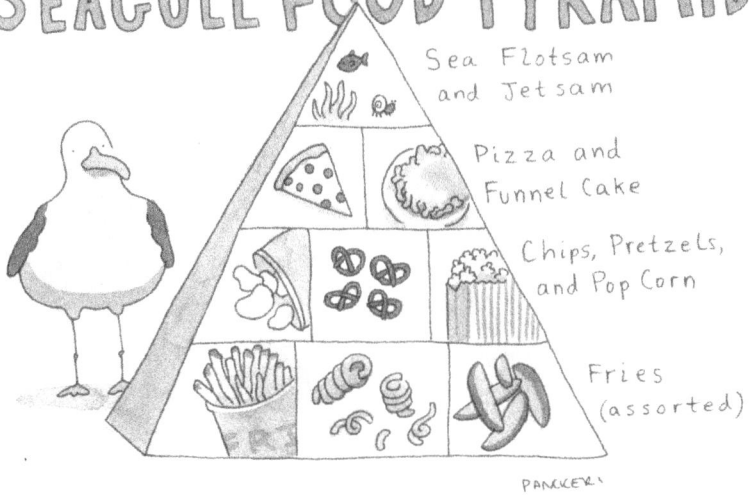

SEAGULL FOOD PYRAMID

Sea Flotsam and Jetsam

Pizza and Funnel Cake

Chips, Pretzels, and Pop Corn

Fries (assorted)

PANKERI

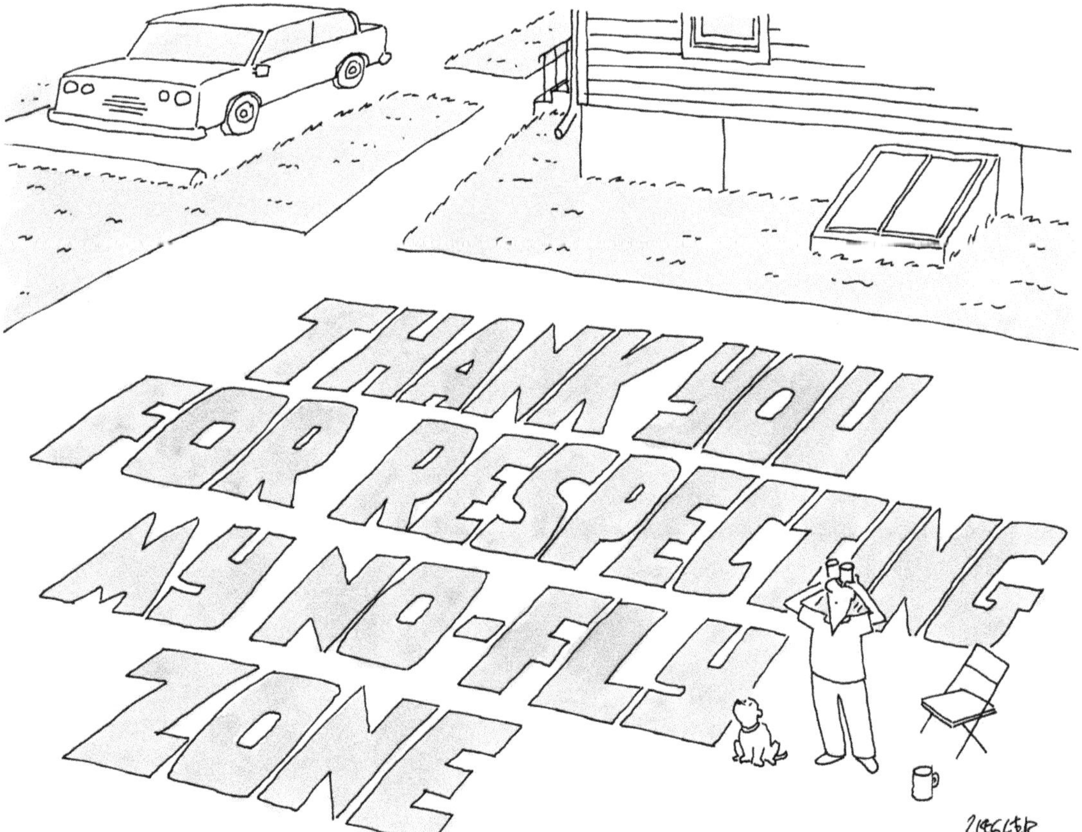
THANK YOU
FOR RESPECTING
MY NO-FLY
ZONE
ZIEGLER

"*I liked him before his tweets got all political.*"

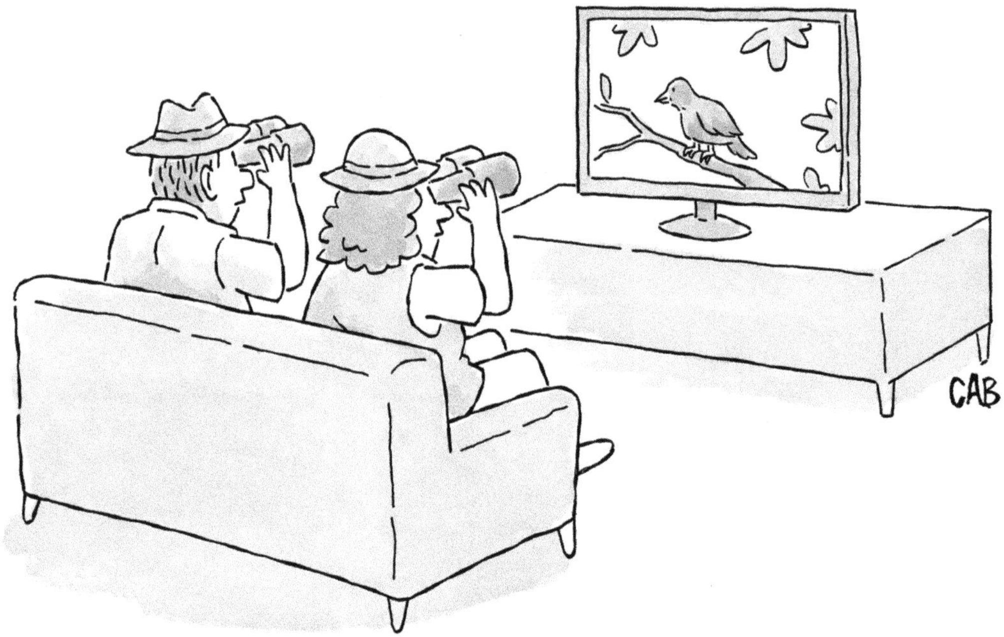
CAB

"They do very well in a talk show format."

"It's getting late, sweetheart. We should probably think about heading back to the Arctic Circle."

"Every generation rebels, dear."

"We can do this the easy way or the Hitchcockian way."

"Tell everyone it was a bigger bird."

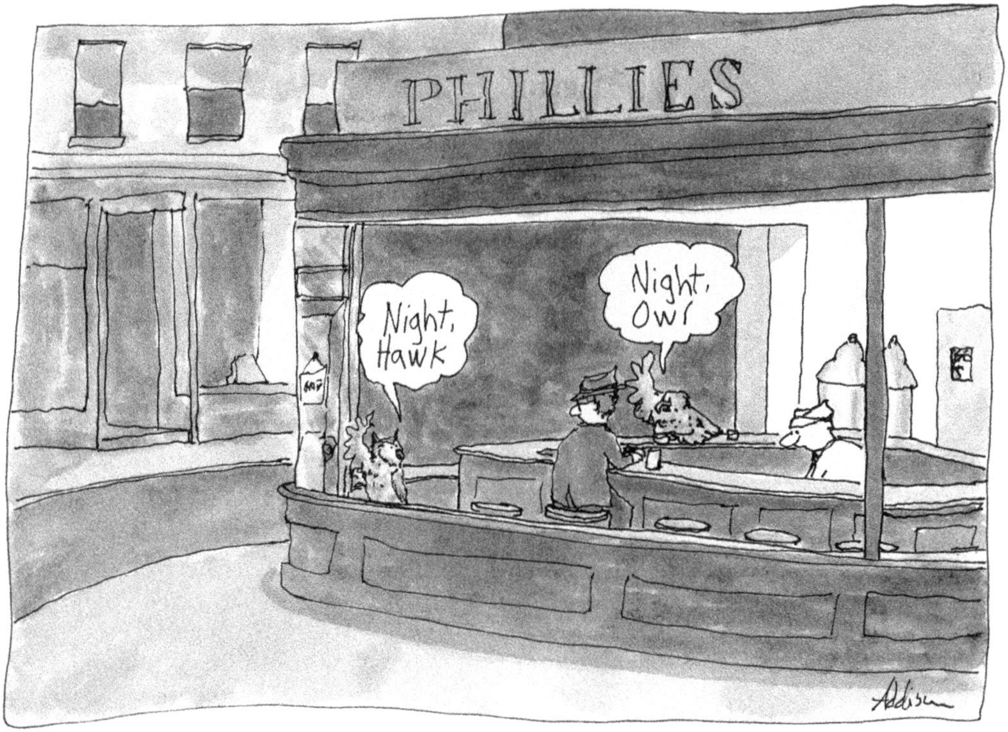
PHILLIES
Night, Hawk
Night, Owl
Addison

"Great first practice. Tomorrow I'll teach you how to land."

"So, how many brands of birds do they make?"

"Have you ever thought about becoming a duck?"

"Oh, ...you know, ...sittin 'on the dock of the bay, ...wastin' time."

"I can usually identify a bird by the song,
but I think he's doing a cover."

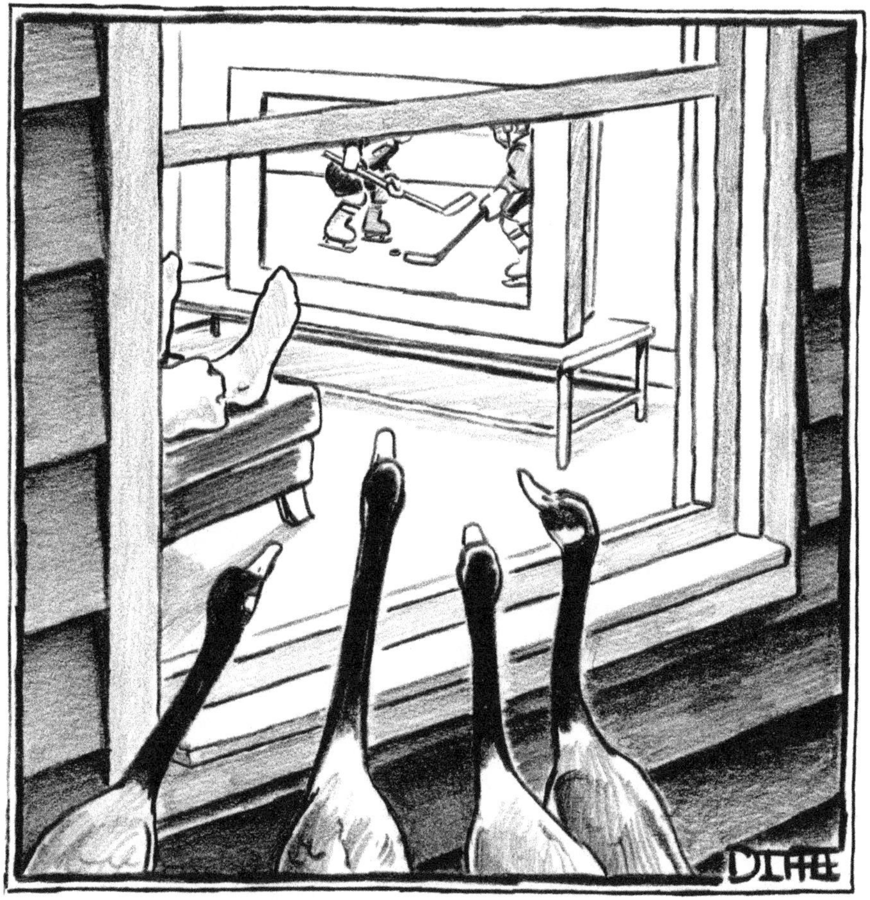
DIFFEE

CANADA GEESE

"You think I just roll our of bed majestic?"

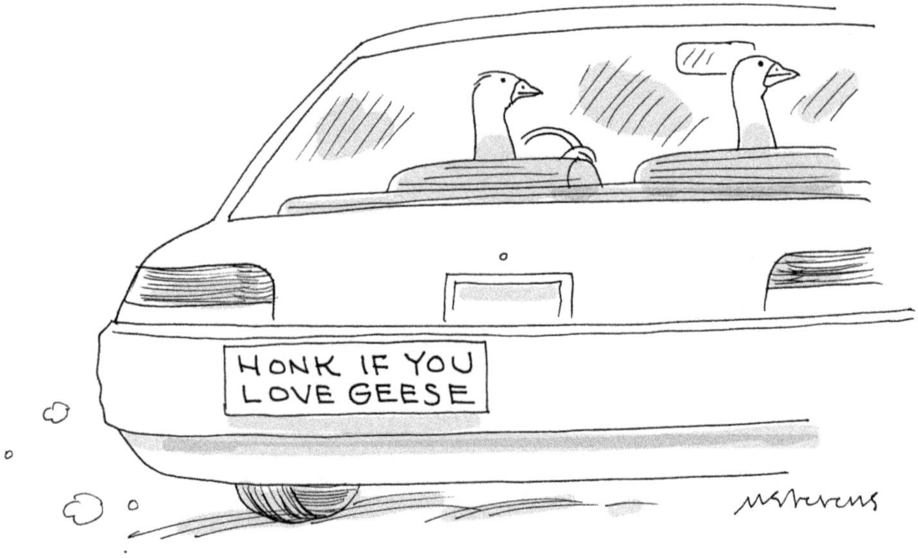
HONK IF YOU
LOVE GEESE

"I think of myself first as an American, then
as a bird, then as a rufous sided towhee."

"Well, then, if and when you do consider
moving, would you let us $\overline{know}$?"

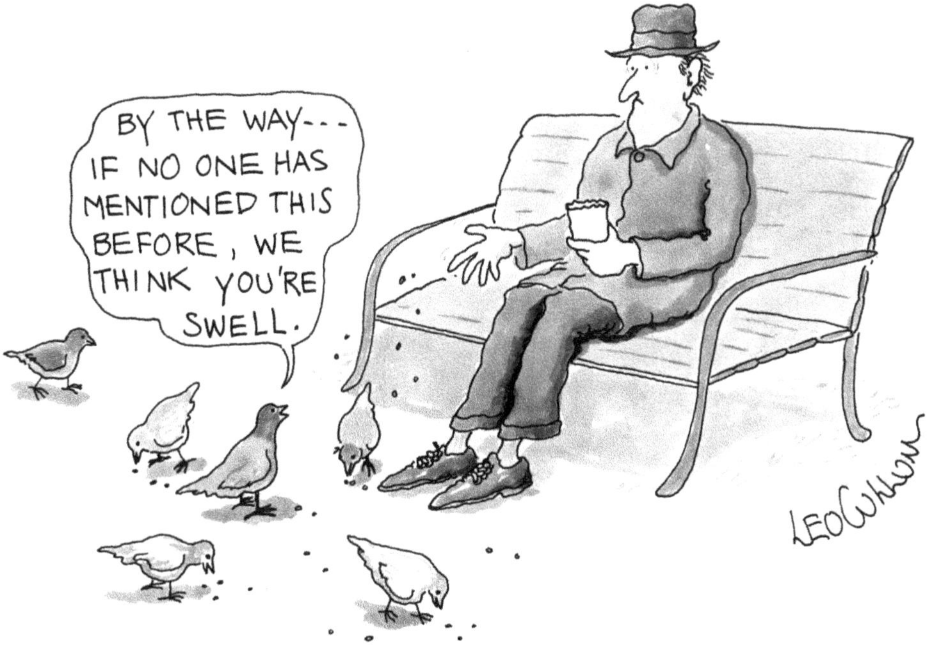
BY THE WAY---
IF NO ONE HAS
MENTIONED THIS
BEFORE, WE
THINK YOU'RE
SWELL.
LEO CULLUM

"What did you think was going to happen when
you filled the feeder with lasagna?"

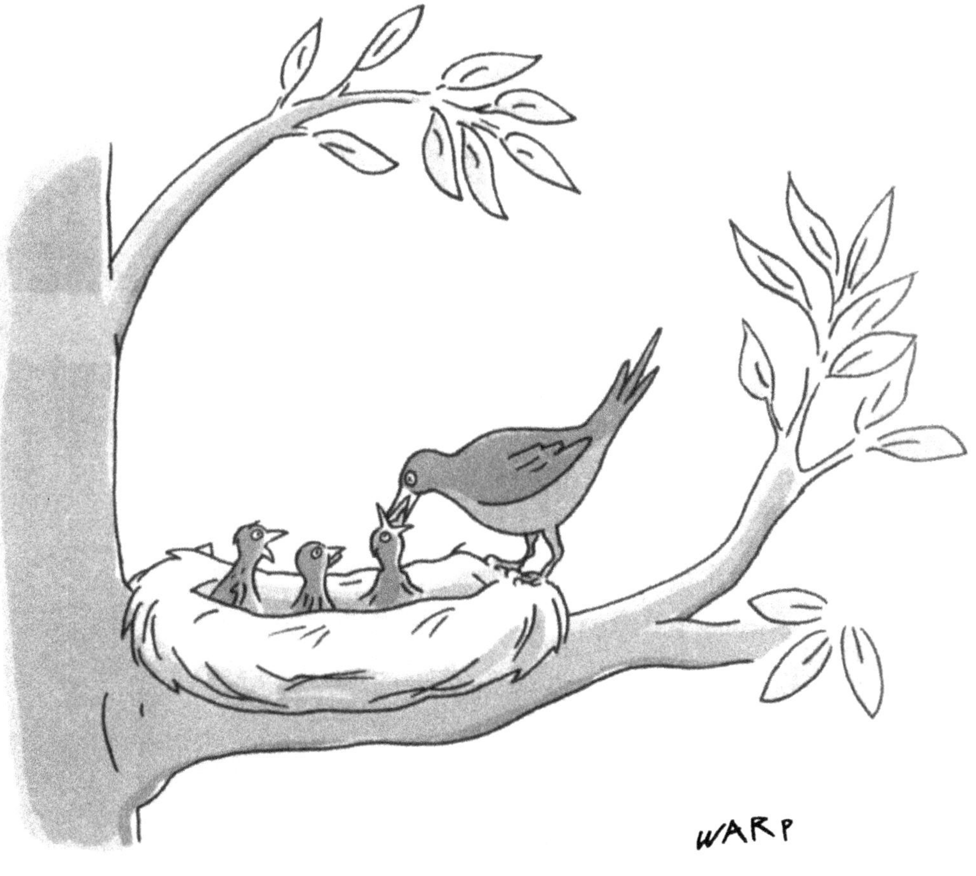
WARP

"Smoothies again?"

BIRDS TALK ABOUT BIRDWATCHERS

– I DON'T CARE WHAT THEY CALL IT– IN MY MIND IT'S STALKING!

TO BE HONEST– THIS IS WHY I DON'T USE THE BIRD BATH!

I'M INVESTING IN BINOCULARS TO SEE HOW _THEY_ LIKE IT!

grahamharrop.com

BIRDWATCHERS MAKING EACH
OTHER PLAYLISTS

E. BLACK

"*Never forget where you came from, son.*"

Hankin

Index of Artists

www.ingramcontent.com/pod-product-compliance
Lightning Source LLC
Chambersburg PA
CBHW040848100426
42813CB00015B/2740